A WORLD OF COMPUTERS AND CODING

CLIVE GIFFORD

WAYLAND
www.waylandbooks.co.uk

First published in Great Britain in 2019 by Wayland

Credits
Editor: Julia Adams
Designer: Rocket Design (East Anglia) Ltd
Picture researcher: Diana Morris

HB ISBN 978 1 5263 0817 7
PB ISBN 978 1 5263 0816 0

Printed in Dubai

Wayland
An imprint of
Hachette Childre
Carmelite House
50 Victoria Embankment
London EC4Y 0DZ

An Hachette UK Company
www.hachette.co.uk

CONTENTS

COMPUTER PLANET

Computers are incredible machines that follow programmed instructions to perform thousands of different tasks – from sending messages via the Internet to controlling a driverless car or running giant factories. Whether on Earth or in space, it's impossible to imagine life without these extraordinary devices, which come in all shapes and sizes.

SMALL AND SIMPLE

Raspberry Pi is a small, cheap computer, barely bigger than a credit card. It's used by people to build and run projects, such as making their own robot.

COMPUTER CONTROL

Many of the systems people rely on every day are controlled by computers. They help forecast the weather, allow people to use electronic banking, control road and rail traffic and guide aircraft.

Computers help air traffic controllers at Sofia Airport in Bulgaria handle over 57,000 plane take-offs and landings every year.

IN SPACE

Computers control the operations of the International Space Station (ISS) and are fitted to robots that explore space, such as the Curiosity Mars Rover.

Astronaut Peggy Whitson controls one of the ISS's robot arms using a touchscreen computer.

COMPUTER NETWORKS

Many computers can communicate with each other via a computer network. The biggest of all is the Internet, which allows billions of machines to link to each other. Smartphones and tablets can access the Internet to view social media, send emails and stream videos and movies.

CHIPPED CATS AND DIGITAL DOGS

Computer technology is even found inside many pets. A pet microchip is injected under the skin of the animal. It contains details of the pet's identity, which can be retrieved when a scanner is waved close to the animal.

GAMES GALORE

Computers can entertain by offering incredible games to play. Many are played on tablets or smartphones. Others are enjoyed on dedicated gaming computers (consoles) such as the Xbox 360 or PlayStation 4, which plug into a television or monitor screen. One game, Minecraft, has sold a staggering 122 million copies worldwide.

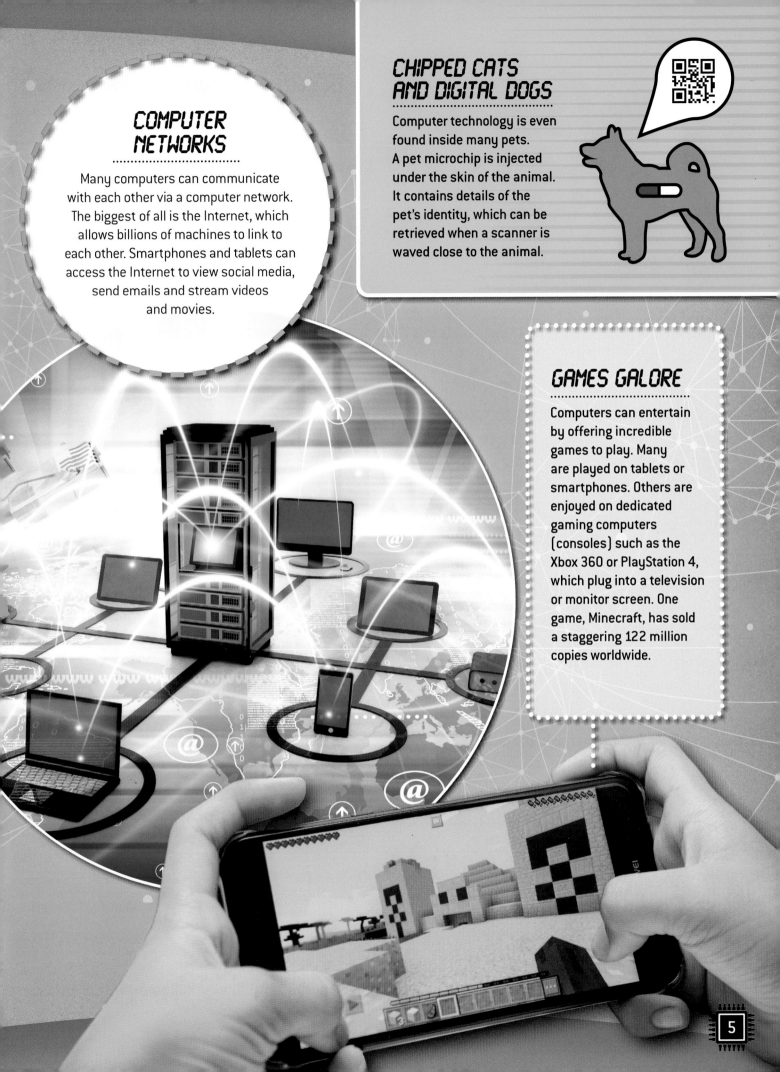

EARLY CALCULATORS

People counted using their fingers for thousands of years. As industry and science advanced in the seventeenth and eighteenth centuries, simple mechanical calculators were invented to help make arithmetic easier. These were the first steps towards modern computers.

ADDING MACHINE

Blaise Pascal was still a teenager when he had to work with his father who collected taxes. All the adding up had to be done by hand and Pascal's inquisitive mind wondered if a machine could help. At the age of 19, in 1642, he unveiled his mechanical calculator – the Pascaline.

ABACUS

The abacus has been used for over 2,000 years to help speed up counting and calculations. Abacuses consist of rows of beads (each representing a number) on wires or rods. The beads can be moved up or down to help perform sums.

BRASS BOX

The Pascaline was housed in a brass box. Inside, the gears and levers could add two numbers together.

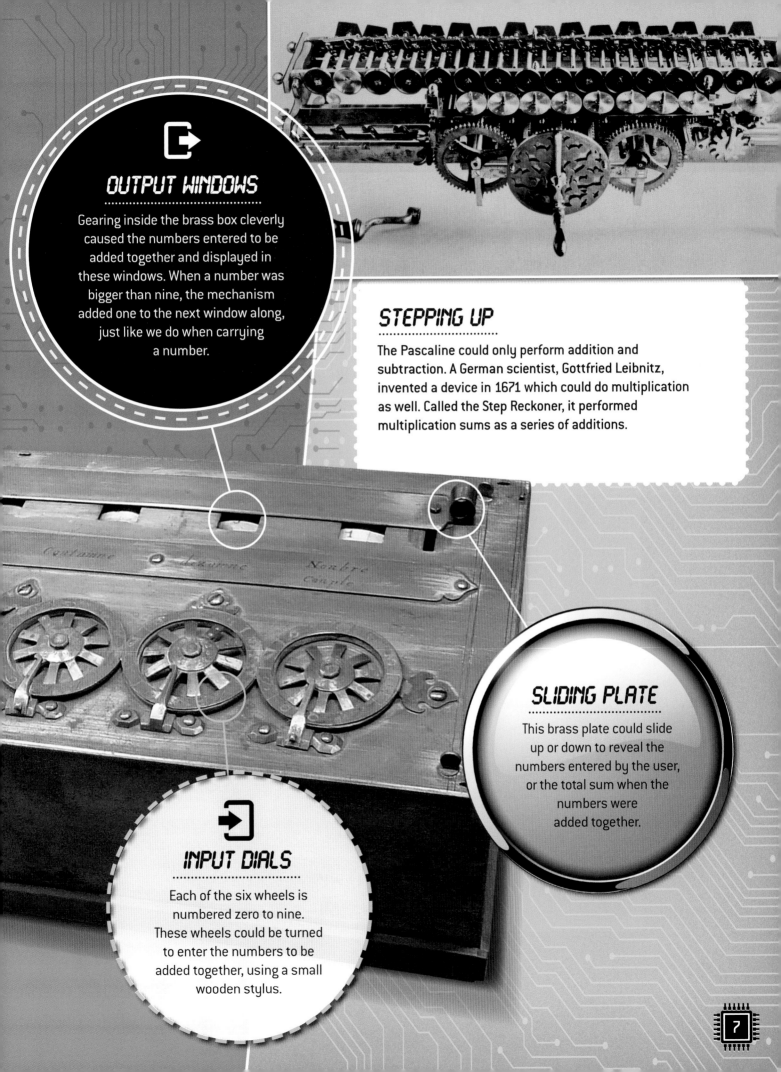

OUTPUT WINDOWS

Gearing inside the brass box cleverly caused the numbers entered to be added together and displayed in these windows. When a number was bigger than nine, the mechanism added one to the next window along, just like we do when carrying a number.

STEPPING UP

The Pascaline could only perform addition and subtraction. A German scientist, Gottfried Leibnitz, invented a device in 1671 which could do multiplication as well. Called the Step Reckoner, it performed multiplication sums as a series of additions.

SLIDING PLATE

This brass plate could slide up or down to reveal the numbers entered by the user, or the total sum when the numbers were added together.

INPUT DIALS

Each of the six wheels is numbered zero to nine. These wheels could be turned to enter the numbers to be added together, using a small wooden stylus.

BABBAGE'S ENGINES

Tired of using books of mathematical tables that were full of errors, Charles Babbage (1791–1871) vowed to build machines to perform calculations more accurately. Although not completed in his lifetime, Babbage's Difference Engines and his design for an Analytical Engine were the forerunners of modern computers.

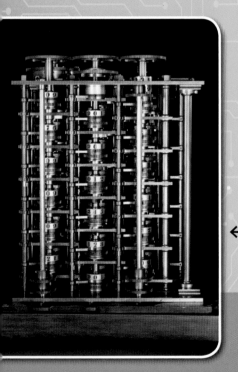

One-seventh of Babbage's first Difference Engine was built in 1832. It featured hundreds of brass parts and still works to this day.

THE DIFFERENCE ENGINE NO. 2

Babbage designed a second Difference Engine in the 1840s. In 1991, the Science Museum in London unveiled their engine, built from Babbage's blueprints. It stood 3.4 m long, 2.1 m high, weighed over 3 tonnes — and worked!

PRECISION PARTS

More than 8,000 bronze, iron and steel parts went into the machine. These all had to be made to precise measurements or the calculator wouldn't work. Babbage had trouble having all these parts made with accuracy during his lifetime.

CALCULATING COLUMNS

Each column of brass gears and wheels stored a decimal number. The gears meshed together and moved when the engine performed arithmetic.

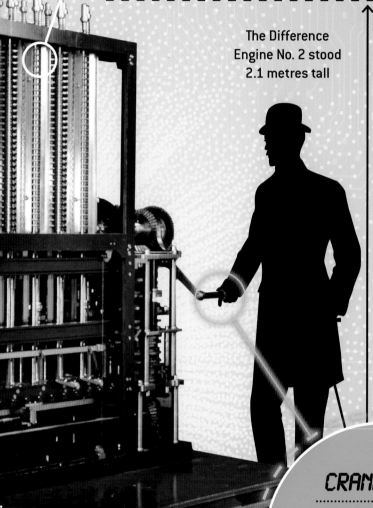

The Difference Engine No. 2 stood 2.1 metres tall

THE FIRST PROGRAMMER

Babbage's friend, Ada, Countess of Lovelace (pictured above), was a gifted amateur mathematician. Babbage called her 'the Enchantress of Numbers'. In 1842, she wrote a series of instructions for the Analytical Engine to solve a set of maths problems. This is regarded as the world's first computer program.

CRANK IT UP

Electricity was not available to Babbage (see right), so his machine was powered by turning this hand crank to move its parts.

Charles Babbage

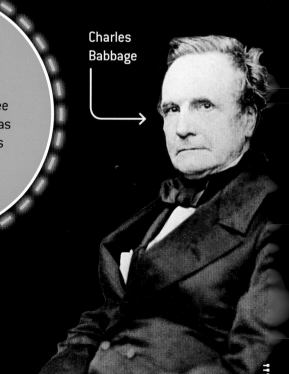

THE ENGINE'S OUTPUT

The results of the engine's calculations could be printed onto paper using black ink. The output could also be pressed into soft material for printing plates, so lots of copies could be produced.

A MATTTER OF LOGIC

Computers work by accepting data or commands (input). They then make calculations and decisions (processing) and finally show the results of their work (output). Breakthroughs in how machines accepted input and made decisions lead to the first working computers of the twentieth century.

ON AND OFF

Computers use the base-two number system, called binary. In binary, there are only two numbers – one and zero. These correspond to whether an input or output is on (1) or off (0). In digital computers, binary numbers are represented by electric signals flowing round the computer's circuits.

DECISION MAKERS

Computers use simple comparisons to help make decisions, such as whether one number is bigger than the other. At the heart of these decisions is something called Boolean logic. It was invented by English mathematician George Boole (1815–64) and works well with the binary number system. Boolean logic is used by devices in computers known as logic gates to make simple 'on' (represented by the number 1) or 'off' (0) decisions. The three common logic gates are AND, NOT and OR (see right).

'NOT' GATE

This gate makes the output the opposite of the input. So, if the input was on (1), the output will be off (0).

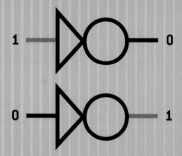

'AND' GATE

An AND gate has two inputs. If both inputs are on (they each equal 1) then the output will be on. If neither or only one of the inputs is on, then the output will be off.

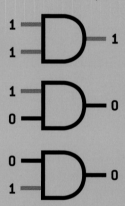

'OR' GATE

An OR gate also has two inputs and if either is on, then the output will be on.

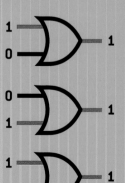

FIRST WORKING COMPUTER

German civil engineer Konrad Zuse (1910–95) built the first working mechanical computer in 1938. The Z1 accepted punched strips of film as input and used binary numbers and Boolean logic to make its calculations and decisions.

← Konrad Zuse

The Z1 had around 20,000 parts and was destroyed in 1943. In 1986, Zuse had the machine (above) rebuilt.

Zuse's Z3 computer used 2,000 switches called relays to help perform calculations. It weighed around one tonne.

ENIAC

One of the very first successful programmable computers was almost the size of a basketball court. The Electronic Numerical Integrator and Computer (ENIAC) ran in the US from 1945 to 1955 and was nicknamed 'Giant Brain'. Designed to calculate the paths of artillery gun shells, it would end up being used for all sorts of tasks, including atomic energy, maths and forecasting the weather.

THE 'GIANT BRAIN'

SPEEDY CALCULATIONS

The computer could make up to 5,000 arithmetic operations a second. This is deadly slow compared to today's PCs, which can perform more than 20 billion per second. It was, however, a considerable improvement on human speed. A job that would have taken people 12 hours or more, could be completed by ENIAC in 30 seconds.

HUMAN COMPUTERS

ENIAC had to be rewired every time it ran a new program – a task that could take two days. A team of six female mathematicians called 'Computers' had to move thousands of plugs and wires.

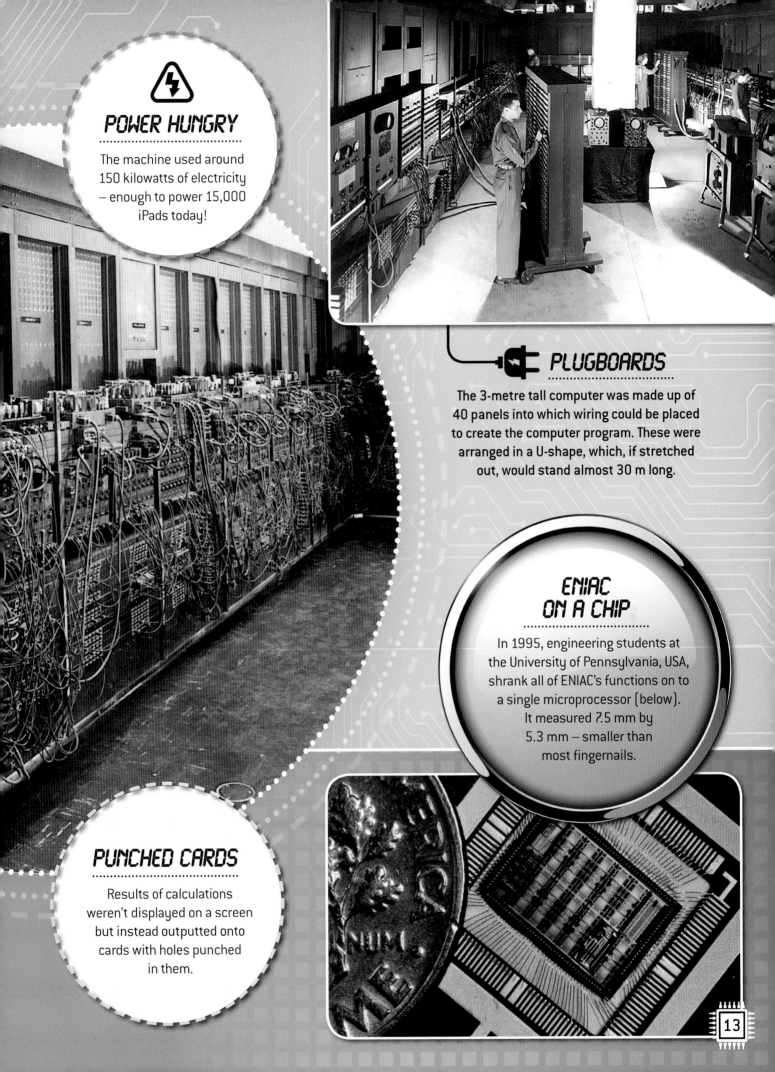

POWER HUNGRY

The machine used around 150 kilowatts of electricity — enough to power 15,000 iPads today!

PLUGBOARDS

The 3-metre tall computer was made up of 40 panels into which wiring could be placed to create the computer program. These were arranged in a U-shape, which, if stretched out, would stand almost 30 m long.

ENIAC ON A CHIP

In 1995, engineering students at the University of Pennsylvania, USA, shrank all of ENIAC's functions on to a single microprocessor (below). It measured 7.5 mm by 5.3 mm — smaller than most fingernails.

PUNCHED CARDS

Results of calculations weren't displayed on a screen but instead outputted onto cards with holes punched in them.

OFF TO WORK

The 1950s was when computers left laboratories and military bases and were used by businesses and other organisations for the first time. These early computers may have been cumbersome and expensive, but they often proved faster than calculating by hand, and paved the way for modern business computing.

UNIVAC 1

The American makers of ENIAC developed the UNIVAC series of computers for business. UNIVAC 1 (shown right) debuted in 1951. More than 40 of these machines were built and used by insurance and utilities companies as well as the US population census. One UNIVAC went against opinion polls to predict successfully that Dwight Eisenhower would win the 1952 US Presidential election. Its final vote prediction of 438 to 93 was less than 1 per cent out.

CONTROL STATION

The computer was programmed from this control station. Meanwhile, other people typed in data on machines which converted their input into magnetic tape.

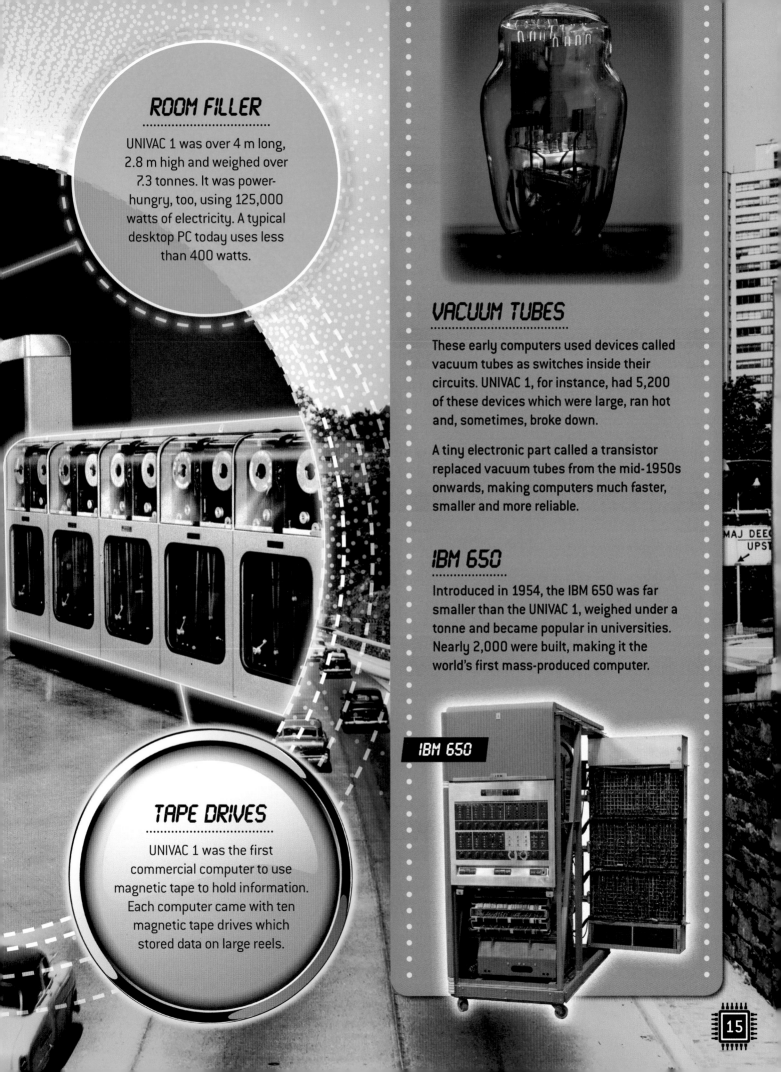

ROOM FILLER

UNIVAC 1 was over 4 m long, 2.8 m high and weighed over 7.3 tonnes. It was power-hungry, too, using 125,000 watts of electricity. A typical desktop PC today uses less than 400 watts.

VACUUM TUBES

These early computers used devices called vacuum tubes as switches inside their circuits. UNIVAC 1, for instance, had 5,200 of these devices which were large, ran hot and, sometimes, broke down.

A tiny electronic part called a transistor replaced vacuum tubes from the mid-1950s onwards, making computers much faster, smaller and more reliable.

IBM 650

Introduced in 1954, the IBM 650 was far smaller than the UNIVAC 1, weighed under a tonne and became popular in universities. Nearly 2,000 were built, making it the world's first mass-produced computer.

IBM 650

TAPE DRIVES

UNIVAC 1 was the first commercial computer to use magnetic tape to hold information. Each computer came with ten magnetic tape drives which stored data on large reels.

COMPILERS

Programming early computers was desperately slow and tedious work until computer languages were invented to speed things up. A key stage towards these languages was the creation of compiler programs. These act as translators, converting the computer language into code that the computer's processor understands.

HIGH-LEVEL LANGUAGE

Computer languages such as Scratch (see page 58), Python and BASIC give programmers lots of easy-to-use programming terms, like PRINT and ADD, to write their programs with, but a computer's processor does not recognise the language's commands.

1

HOW A COMPILER WORKS

A computer's central processing unit (see page 22) can only understand instructions in machine code. This is usually in binary (the base-two number system), so results in a massive stream of ones and zeroes.

COMPILER CHAMPION

Grace Hopper (1906–92; pictured left) worked on one of the first computers, the Harvard Mark I, during the Second World War. She was then involved in developing the UNIVAC 1 computer (see pages 14–15). A programming pioneer, Hopper and her team created the A-0 compiler in 1952. It turned maths equations and programming instructions into machine code that would run on the UNIVAC 1.

A giant container ship docks in New York. The programs that help direct container shipping movement and loading are often written in COBOL.

LONG-RUNNING LANGUAGE

Using new versions of their compiler, Hopper and her team created a computer language for businesses called FLOW-MATIC. In 1959, it formed the basis of COBOL, a language still used today in programs run by air traffic control, container ship ports and in finance. Many bank cash dispensers, for example, are still programmed in COBOL.

COMPILER

The program is run in a compiler. This takes all the program's instructions and information that have been input in high-level language and converts them into simple machine code that the processor of a computer understands.

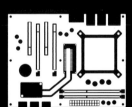

2

PROCESSOR

Once the program has been compiled into machine code, it can then be run on the computer.

```
010011010
001101001
00011001
0101110
0010001
```

3

HARD DISK DRIVE

Hard disk drives store much of the world's computer data. These computing workhorses are rarely thought about, but are phenomenal examples of engineering. They hold huge amounts of information which can be retrieved quickly.

ACTUATOR ARM

This moves in and out to locate a particular sector of a platter. A high-performance hard disk drive can perform this task in less than 10 thousandth of a second.

READ/WRITE HEADS

Found on the end of the arms, the write heads change the magnetic field of part of the platter to store data. The platters keep storing the data, even when the hard drive or the computer it is connected to is switched off. The gap between the heads and a platter is incredibly small – around 5,000 times thinner than a human hair.

DISK CONTROLLER

This circuit board contains the parts that control the flow of data to and from the platters. It regulates the process of saving, retrieving and deleting files from the hard disk.

SPINDLE

An electric motor turns this spindle, which spins the platters at very high speeds. Many hard disk drives run at 7,200 revolutions per minute (rpm). That's equal to a speed of around 120 km/h.

PLATTERS

These discs are made of metal or glass and coated in a magnetic material on both sides. A computer file is split up and stored in different places, known as sectors, on a platter.

DISK DEBUT

In 1956, the world's first hard disk drive debuted – the IBM 350 Disk File (see above). It was the size of a double freezer, weighed 1 tonne and could only be moved by a fork lift truck! The entire machine could hold around 3.75 megabytes (MB) of data.

The largest capacity hard drives today are the size of a small book and can hold 4 million times as much data – up to 12 terabytes (TB).

In data centres, row upon row of server computers all store a huge amount of data on large hard disks.

INPUT DEVICES

We use input devices to enter data or instructions into a computer system. Keyboards, touchscreens and games controllers, such as a gamepad or joystick, are all common input devices. So is the computer mouse first developed in 1963 by Douglas Engelbart and Bill English.

THE FIRST MOUSE

Made of wood and containing just one small button, the first mouse had two large wheels set at right angles to each other. When moved across a surface, the amount the wheels turned was converted into instructions to move a cursor around a screen.

OTHER INPUT DEVICES

Graphics tablets are pressure-sensitive pads. Users can draw or write on the pad using a stylus. The stylus' movements are translated by computer programs into on-screen actions, such as erasing or shading.

Document scanners turn a physical document such as a printed photo or book page into a digital file that can be handled by a computer.

INSIDE AN OPTICAL MOUSE

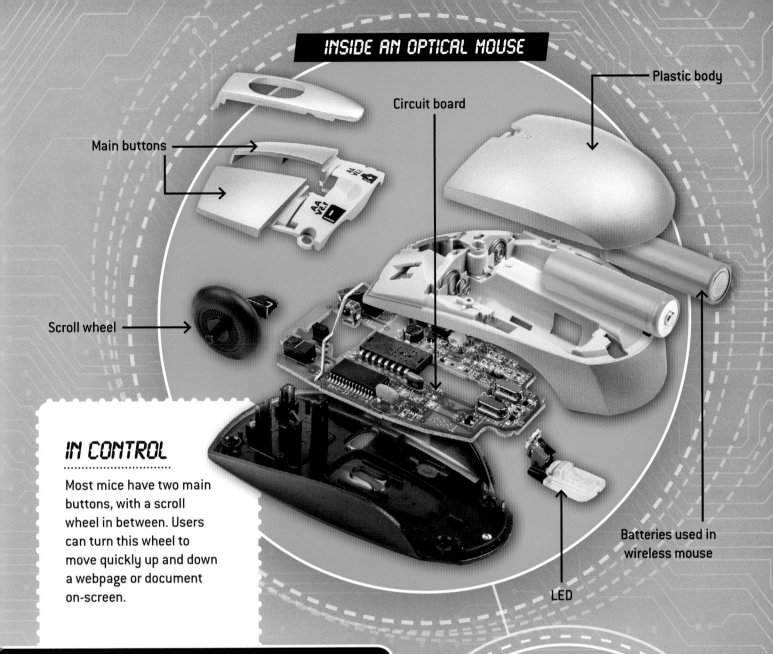

Plastic body

Circuit board

Main buttons

Scroll wheel

Batteries used in wireless mouse

LED

IN CONTROL

Most mice have two main buttons, with a scroll wheel in between. Users can turn this wheel to move quickly up and down a webpage or document on-screen.

For the Kinect controller for the Xbox 360 and One games consoles, you are the input device! Your movements are captured and measured by the Kinect sensor bar and turned into in-game actions.

OPTICAL MOUSE

An optical mouse uses electronics rather than wheels to calculate its position. Light emitting diodes (LEDs) shine narrow beams of red light on to the surface beneath the mouse. The light bounces back and strikes a device on the bottom of the mouse, called a photocell. This registers the angle at which the light hits it and sends a signal to the mouse's processor chip. The processor turns the signals into data about how far, fast and in what direction the mouse is moving.

21

MICROPROCESSORS

Microprocessors are the 'brains' of computers, smartphones and other digital devices. They have thousands or millions of microscopic electronics parts and circuits. These perform calculations and decisions, as well as controlling other parts of the device.

SHRINKING CIRCUITS

The invention of the transistor saw circuits shrink in size until, by the 1960s, they could be crammed on to a tiny wafer of silicon – a silicon chip. Some microcomputers of the time used a number of these chips linked together to perform their processing. In 1971, the Intel 4004, with all of a computer's processing functions on a single chip, went on sale for the first time.

This Intel i7-6800K contains over 1.7 billion transistors.

TRANSISTOR COUNT

As circuits shrank further and more and more transistors were crammed on to them, the power of microprocessors increased. In 1993, the first Intel Pentium microprocessor, used in many personal computers (PCs), was released. It contained 3.1 million transistors, while 21 years later, the Apple A8 chip used in the iPhone 6 contained 2 billion.

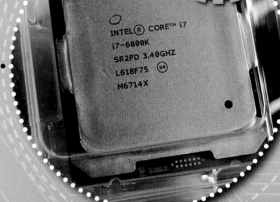

The Intel 4004 was smaller than most fingernails, yet contained 2,300 transistors.

EMBEDDED COMPUTING

Microprocessors don't just turn up in computers and smartphones. Millions are found embedded in a vast range of other devices they control – from digital cameras and DVD players to 'smart' watches and washing machines.

MAKING MICROPROCESSORS

SPOTLESS

It takes hundreds of complicated steps to make a microprocessor, many of which take place inside specialist 'clean rooms' where the air is hundreds of times purer than in a hospital's operating theatre.

SILICON SLICES

Chemically treated silicon ingots are produced, then cut into thin slices. Each will contain many chips.

INCREDIBLE ETCHING

A complete plan of the microprocessor's circuits and components is reduced down again and again before it can be etched microscopically on to each chip. A transistor in a modern microprocessor can be 10,000 times thinner than a human hair.

C AND C++

Computers are programmed using one of a number of languages, such as Java, Python or Ruby. The C programming language was first developed between 1969 and 1973 at Bell Labs in the USA. It remains popular to this day, used on computers and digital devices as varied as smartphones and fighter jets.

CODED AND COMPILED

A program is written in C by a coder. It then has to be run through a compiler (see pages 16–17) to turn it into a form that the computer can use. The eventual code runs fast and can be easily reworked and re-compiled to run on different types of devices.

OPERATING SYSTEMS

An operating system is the collection of programs that control a computer or digital device. Some, such as Linux and Android (the operating system found on most of the world's tablets and smartphones), are written in C.

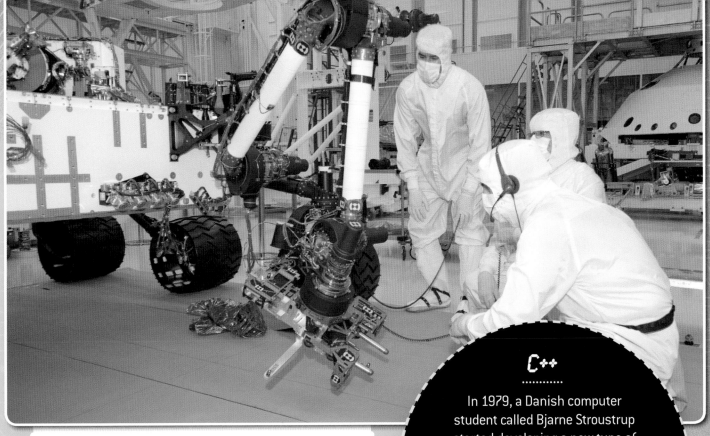

C IN CURIOSITY

NASA's Curiosity (shown above) is a roving robot explorer, travelling around the surface of the planet Mars. Programs written in C, and made up of over 2 million lines of code, help control Curiosity's robotic arm, as well as all its experiment packages and moving parts.

C++

In 1979, a Danish computer student called Bjarne Stroustrup started developing a new type of C. It become known as C++ and proved powerful and versatile. Many web browsers were written in C++, as was much of the Google search engine and the programs that control many car sat navs.

GREAT FOR GRAPHICS

It takes a lot of lines of code to complete a program in C++, but the result is powerful. It is often used for fast-moving graphics such as those found in action games. World of Warcraft, for example, contains over 5.5 million lines of code, mostly written in C++.

DIGITAL CAMERAS

Digital cameras record images as data files. The images can be printed, stored on a computer's hard disk drive or sent to other digital devices instantly.

TAKING A PICTURE

1 FRONT VIEW

FLASH!

A flash provides a brief burst of light to scenes too dark to be snapped otherwise.

LIGHT SENSOR

In the camera body, the light strikes the sensor chip, which converts it into electrical signals. Microchips then process the signals into an image file that is saved in memory.

GOPRO

This GoPro Hero camera is shockproof and waterproof. It can be mounted on bikes, canoes and helmets to produce exciting action videos.

CAMERAS EVERYWHERE

SCREEN TEST

The screen can be used to display photos already taken or display menus of options for the user to select from.

MAKING MEMORIES

Most digicams have some built-in memory, but can also accept portable memory cards capable of storing thousands of images.

THROUGH THE LENS

This gathers in light and focuses it on the sensor inside the camera. Many digital camera lenses can zoom in to show distant objects larger in the photo.

SMARTPHONE

Smartphone cameras are tiny (less than 1 cm square), but can produce detailed images, thanks to the smartphone's powerful microprocessor.

DRONE

Digital cameras are fitted to remote-controlled flying robots, known as drones. Drone cameras are used for security, to make surveys of land below and to take stunning aerial photos.

LET THE GAMES BEGIN!

The first computer games reached arcades in the early 1970s. They were mostly silent and black and white. But as computer technology and game design advanced, arcade games became fast, colourful, noisy and action-packed.

NAMCO

Rally X in 1980 was the first arcade game to feature a musical soundtrack. Its makers, Japanese company Namco, also produced Galaxians and, in 1981, the smash hit Pac-Man. Over 400,000 Pac-Man consoles were built – the most of any arcade game.

PONG

In 1972, Atari created the first Pong arcade game using parts from a launderette washing machine, a milk carton and a TV. More than 30,000 Pong machines would eventually be produced.

Pong was one of the first tennis bat and ball computer games.

ARCADE BOOM

Japanese companies Taito and Namco revolutionised arcade gaming with fast action and colour graphics. Released in 1978, Taito's Space Invaders (left) was the first shooter game where the targets – the alien invaders – shot back. It was also the first game to save and display a high score.

RISE OF RHYTHM

In 1997, Konami invented Beatmania, where players act as DJs, mixing songs and beats in time. It sparked a series of rhythm games (see above), where players step on pressure-sensitive squares as they light up. They need to do this in time with the music, copying the dance moves displayed on-screen.

ATARI 2600

Nolan Bushnell and Ted Dabney had already designed arcade games before they developed the first popular gaming computer for the home. Launched in 1977 as the Atari Video Computer System (VCS), it later became known as the Atari 2600.

CARTRIDGES

Games were stored on plastic cartridges which clipped into a slot. The cartridges contained just 4 kilobytes (KB) of storage for games, so the games had to be programmed well to work within such a small amount of memory.

JOYSTICK

The console came with two sets of controllers: a pair of paddles (far right) with a dial you turned left or right, and joysticks (below). The joysticks could move up, down, left or right, but not diagonally, and had a single fire button.

COLOUR SWITCH

Users moved this switch to tell the console whether they were using a colour or black and white television.

Donkey Kong

TOP·000000
[M][BONUS][L]
[O][3600][I]

DEGREE OF DIFFICULTY

Each gamer could select an easy or hard level of game difficulty using this switch.

paddle

BEFORE AND AFTER ATARI

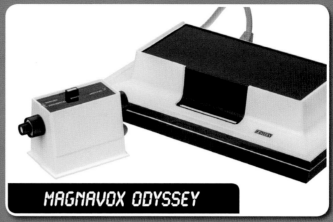

MAGNAVOX ODYSSEY

Ralph Baer made the first home games console in 1967. A version of it went on sale as the Magnavox Odyssey. Most of the console's simple black and white games were controlled by a box with two dials and one button.

XBOX ONE

Packed with powerful microprocessors, modern consoles today, such as this Xbox One, can run fast, complex games with amazing graphics. The Xbox's 500-GB hard disk drive gives it 4.2 thousand million times more memory than an Atari 2600.

MULTIPLE CARTRIDGES

Atari cartridges included games popular in arcades such as Asteroids, Space Invaders, Pac-Man and Pitfall! – one of the first successful platform games. More than 450 different games were produced for the machine.

space invaders

ASTEROIDS

missile command™ R

FROGGER™

THE HOME COMPUTER BOOM

Next-to-no-one one had a computer at home until the arrival of a wave of small computers powered by microprocessors in the late 1970s and early 1980s. The first were kits that electronics hobbyists had to build themselves. Then came machines like the Apple II, Commodore 64, Sinclair ZX81 and Sinclair Spectrum, which were ready-built.

APPLE II

TV SCREEN

A socket allowed the computer to be connected to a regular TV screen. The computer's graphics were in colour, but made up of large blocks, as the resolution was low.

Starwars
P/N A2T0002X

>Load
16K

‹1978

600-2013-00   apple computer inc.

ON TAPE

Computer programs were stored on audio cassette tapes, played on a regular tape deck to load them on to the computer. This could take nine or ten minutes for a bigger program!

CASSETTE HEROES

Thousands of people learned to program for the first time and wrote and sold their own programs and games to others on cassette. More than 24,000 different programs were created for the ZX Spectrum, for example.

KEYBOARD

Most early home computers contained a built-in keyboard and no mouse or other input device. Many people typed in all the instructions for programs by referring to books and magazines.

BASIC

Most home computers of the era were programmable using the BASIC computer language. This contained instructions in English language, such as 'GOTO' meaning 'jump to a different line of code'.

··· COMPETITORS ···

COMMODORE 64

While other home computers could only manage beeps, the Commodore 64 had a dedicated sound chip that could play music.

SINCLAIR ZX81

The ZX81 could only display black and white. It came with just 1 kilobyte (KB) of RAM inside for program storage.

SINCLAIR SPECTRUM

The ZX81's successor weighed just 550 g, had at least 16 times more memory and displayed programs in colour.

SUPERCOMPUTERS

Supercomputers are particularly powerful computers capable of performing at searing speeds. They're used for large, complex computing tasks, such as modelling how atoms and molecules work, weather forecasting and running huge simulations of how explosions occur.

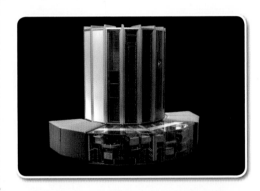

CRAY 1

The Cray 1 (left), designed by Seymour Cray in 1976, is thought of as the first supercomputer. It contained more than 90 km of wiring and was the fastest computer in the world for five years. It could run at a speed of 130 megaflops. That's 130 million calculations every second.

SPEEDY SUPERCOMPUTING

Titan can perform at speeds of over 17,000 teraflops. That is 17,000 thousand billion calculations every second.

A supercomputer runs a detailed simulation of an earthquake from the past.

PARALLEL PROCESSING

Many supercomputers work incredibly fast by splitting a major task into lots of different parts and working on all of these parts at the same time. This is known as parallel processing and requires supercomputers to have many processors all running together.

200 CABINETS

The Titan supercomputer contains 18,688 processors and a further 18,688 graphics card processors, all housed in 200 cabinets that cover an area of 440 square metres – about 1½ times the size of a tennis court.

THE TITAN SUPERCOMPUTER

Located at Oak Ridge National Laboratory in the USA, Titan was completed in 2013 and was built to run lots of different science programs investigating climate change, how materials form and detailed modelling of the entire Milky Way.

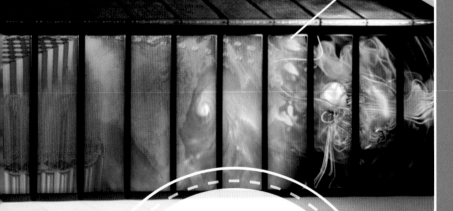

FASTEST OF ALL

Supercomputers kept on speeding up, and in 2016, the Sunway TaihuLight (right) became the world's most powerful supercomputer. Designed in China to investigate how the Universe began, it contains 40,960 processors. These help give it a top speed of 93,000 teraflops – that's an incredible 58 million times faster than an Apple iPad 2 tablet.

SUPER STORAGE

All those processors need a lot of storage and Titan can hold 40,000 terabytes (TB). Most home computers have just one or two terabytes of storage.

IBM PERSONAL COMPUTER

Few small businesses used computers until the arrival in 1981 of the IBM 5510 personal computer, or PC for short. Fast and flexible compared to other computers of the time, IBM PCs became very popular with small businesses and home users. Many companies copied IBM's design to produce PC 'clones' and a vast range of computer programs for the machine appeared.

OPERATING SYSTEM

An operating system is a set of programs which control the basic functions of a computer. The IBM PC's original operating system was MS-DOS, created by Paul Allen and Bill Gates of Microsoft.

KEYBOARD

Many computers of the time had a keyboard fitted into the computer's main body. The IBM PC's keyboard featured 83 keys and attached to the computer via a 2m-long curled cord. The keys included 10 function keys that could be programmed to perform different tasks.

COLOUR MONITOR

The PC's colour screen could display 24 lines of text in up to 16 colours.

DOT MATRIX PRINTER

This printer used a head made up of small metal dots which struck an inked ribbon to print characters on to paper. The printer operated at a speed of up to 80 letters or numbers printed per second.

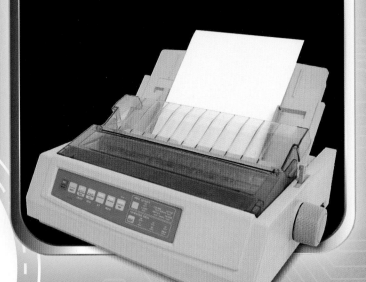

PROCESSOR AND MEMORY

Housed inside the main cabinet was an Intel 8088 microprocessor which controlled the PC. The machine came with just 16 kilobytes (KB) of memory. A 16-GB smartphone today has a million times more memory.

EXPANSION SLOTS

Housed inside the case were five slots that could accept expansion cards. These were printed circuit boards containing electronics which could extend the computer's functions, such as giving the computer extra memory.

FLOPPY DISK DRIVES

Programs could be loaded on to the computer via an audio cassette player or floppy disk drives. These used discs of plastic coated in a magnetic material that were 13.3 cm in diameter.

THE NINTENDO REVOLUTION

Portable computer gaming really took off with the launch of Nintendo's Game Boy console in 1989. Together with its successor, the Game Boy Color, more than 118 million of these machines have been sold. Nintendo's other great games console success, the Wii, was launched in 2006.

GREY SCREEN

The 4.7 cm x 4.3 cm screen could display four shades of grey and had a resolution of 160 × 144 pixels, a tiny fraction of the resolution found on a modern tablet or smartphone.

1 FRONT VIEW

IN CONTROL

The directional controller pad featured four arrows connected to switches, allowing the player to move in-game characters up, down, left and right.

PCB

The printed circuit board contained the console's microprocessor and just 8 KB of random access memory (RAM).

SERIAL PORT

The Game Boy didn't feature wireless communication. An input socket, however, allowed two Game Boys to be connected by a cable so that the players could battle it out in the same game.

Small cartridges contained memory chips that held different games programs. Popular games for the Game Boy included Tetris, Donkey Kong and Super Mario Land.

CH1 1196916

Nintendo GAME BOY.COLOR MODEL NO. CGB-001

RATING : DC3V 0.6W ⓒⓇ 1998 Nintendo
BATTERY : LR6 (AA)x2   Patents issued and Pending. See booklet.
THIS DEVICE COMPLIES WITH PART 15 OF THE FCC RULES. OPERATION IS SUBJECT TO THE FOLLOWING TWO CONDITIONS: (1) THIS DEVICE MAY NOT CAUSE HARMFUL INTERFERENCE, AND (2) THIS DEVICE MUST ACCEPT ANY INTERFERENCE RECEIVED, INCLUDING INTERFERENCE THAT MAY CAUSE UNDESIRED OPERATION. THIS CLASS B DIGITAL APPARATUS MEETS ALL REQUIREMENTS OF THE CANADIAN INTERFERENCE-CAUSING EQUIPMENT REGULATIONS.

MADE IN CHINA   C/CGB-JPN-1   Ⓒ ACN 060 566 083

GAME BOY

BATTERY POWER
....

Four AA batteries fitted into the back of the machine. They provided power for between 15 and 30 hours of gaming.

2 REAR VIEW

← Nintendo Wii

NINTENDO WII
....

Nintendo's most famous home games console was the Wii. It appealed to both gamers and families, with over 900 million games sold. They were all played and controlled, not by a joystick, but by the console's wireless Wii Remote or (Wiimote).

Tim Berners-Lee

THE WORLD WIDE WEB

The World Wide Web was developed by British computer engineer Tim Berners-Lee. He created a program, ENQUIRE, to keep track of everyone working at CERN, a giant set of labs in Switzerland. In 1989–90, he developed this into a system that could link information worldwide.

SO HOW DOES THE WORLD WIDE WEB WORK?

CLIENT COMPUTER

Client sends an HTTP message to a computer running a web server program and asks for a document.

Web server sends a hypermedia HTML document to the client, in this case, the YouTube homepage.

CLIENT COMPUTER

This can be a personal computer, a tablet, smartphone or some other device running a web browser. This program allows users to request a particular webpage by typing in its URL. The program then fetches the webpage and displays it on-screen.

URL

Every document and page on the World Wide Web has its own unique address, known as a URL (Uniform Resource Locator). Typing a URL into a web browser takes you to that webpage.

The very popular web search engine called Google was invented by computer scientists Larry Page (right) and Sergey Brin (far right). The site was named after a googol – the name for the number 1 followed by 100 zeros.

It's hard to imagine now, but the World Wide Web was not an instant success. By June 1993, there were only 130 websites in the whole world. However, numbers started to build, especially as new web browsers allowed users to view graphics. By 2017, there were more than 1.2 billion websites.

WEB SERVER

WEB SERVER

These computers store webpages and make them available to other machines. When a web server receives a request from a client computer, it searches its storage and if it finds the page or file, and sends it back over the Internet to the client.

HTML

Hypertext Mark-Up Language is used to prepare a document so that it can become a webpage and be viewed by anyone, anywhere. A completed webpage is uploaded on to a web server. A website is a collection of webpages.

3D PRINTING

Printing in three dimensions (3D) is possible using 3D printers. These vary in size from tabletop models, used to print action figures in stores, to giant machines capable of printing entire vehicles or buildings.

Component is modelled using a computer aided design (CAD) program.

COMPUTER MODELLING

In order to print a 3D object, the first step is to produce an accurate 3D digital model using computer aided design (CAD) programs. A further program called a slicer produces code that describes the shape of the object, slice by slice. A complex or large object may be made up of thousands of slices. All this coding is sent to the 3D printer as instructions.

PLASTIC FILAMENT

Hobbyist 3D printers use reels of plastic strands called filaments, which an electric motor gradually feeds into the printer. Industrial machines may print using metals, sandstone or carbon fibre.

CONCRETE PRINTING

Using a large 3D printer capable of printing layers of concrete, U.S. company Apis Cor created a house in 24 hours.

PRINT HEAD

The plastic is heated until it is soft and a single layer is released from the print head on to the build plate, a little like an accurate hot glue gun. The process is controlled by the CAD model of the final object sent to the 3D printer.

3D PRINTED PARTS

All sorts of objects can be produced using 3D printing, from toys and made-to-measure artificial body parts, such as dental crowns or prosthetic hands, to vehicle parts. The Airbus A350 WXB airliner, for example, contains more than 1,000 3D-printed parts, while the entire body and chassis of Divergent 3D's Blade supercar are 3D printed.

Finished component on the print bed

2:25:51
61°C
PRINTING

CARRIAGE MECHANISM

This moves the print head repeatedly over the object, building it up layer by thin layer. A typical layer is just 0.1 mm thick, so printing a large object can take many hours. The end result is a perfect replica of the digital model designed on the computer.

BLADE SUPERCAR

HUMAN JAW

SMARTPHONES

Smartphones are effectively powerful and versatile portable computers, all packed into a slim mobile phone. A top 2017 smartphone such as the iPhone X or Samsung S8 possessed more computing power than a giant supercomputer from the early 1990s!

CAPACITIVE TOUCHSCREEN

The whole phone screen is both a display and an input device, thanks to the touchscreen. A small electric charge covers the entire screen. When your finger touches the screen, the charge changes slightly. Sensors detect the change and convert it into instructions such as 'move left', or 'close a window'.

THE FIRST SMARTPHONE

IBM's Simon is considered the first smartphone. It was unveiled in 1992, 15 years before the first iPhone. It had a touchscreen and could handle emails but was heavy, at over 500 g and could only run for an hour before its battery needed recharging.

APP ATTACK

Small programs called apps can be downloaded from the Internet on to the phone. By 2016, there were over 2.4 million different apps available on the Google Play store alone.

VIDEO CALL

Smartphones can establish a connection with another online device to provide live video calls with the help of the phone's camera and microphone.

WHICH WAY UP?

Devices called accelerometers identify which direction a phone is pointing in and can instruct the phone to switch its display between portrait and landscape.

Camera lens

MEMORY

The latest smartphones often possess 32 or 64 GB of internal memory – enough to hold thousands of photos, apps or music tracks. Micro SD cards slide into a slot on many smartphones to provide additional, removable, memory.

MICROPHONE

This device , on the bottom edge of the phone, gathers sound. It's used for voice calls but also in apps such as voice control, which can be used to browse the Internet.

2   REAR VIEW

SECURITY MEASURES

A fingerprint scanner only unlocks the phone when it recognises the fingerprint of the phone owner. Some smartphones also have an iris scanner to do a similar job, as everyone's coloured part of their eye is unique and can be used to identify them.

MAN VERSUS MACHINE

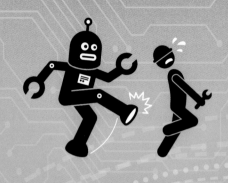

Computers are not built smart — they have to be instructed by programs to perform tasks. But some computers run programs that enable them to learn or use the power of their processors to run through millions of pieces of data and arrive at a decision. Sometimes, in human tests of knowledge and skill, computers win out.

COMPUTER CHAMPS

The first computer program to triumph in a high-level board game championship was Hans Berliner's BKG 9.8 backgammon program, defeating human world champion Luigi Villa in 1979. Since that time, programs have defeated notable champions in Scrabble, draughts and, in 2016, the Chinese strategy game Go.

World scrabble champion David Boys from Canada loses to a computer running a Scrabble playing program called Quackle.

COMPUTER CHESS

The first chess programs ran on giant computers in the 1950s and 1960s. As technology has progressed, chess programs that can challenge good chess players have been coded to run on tablets and smartphones.

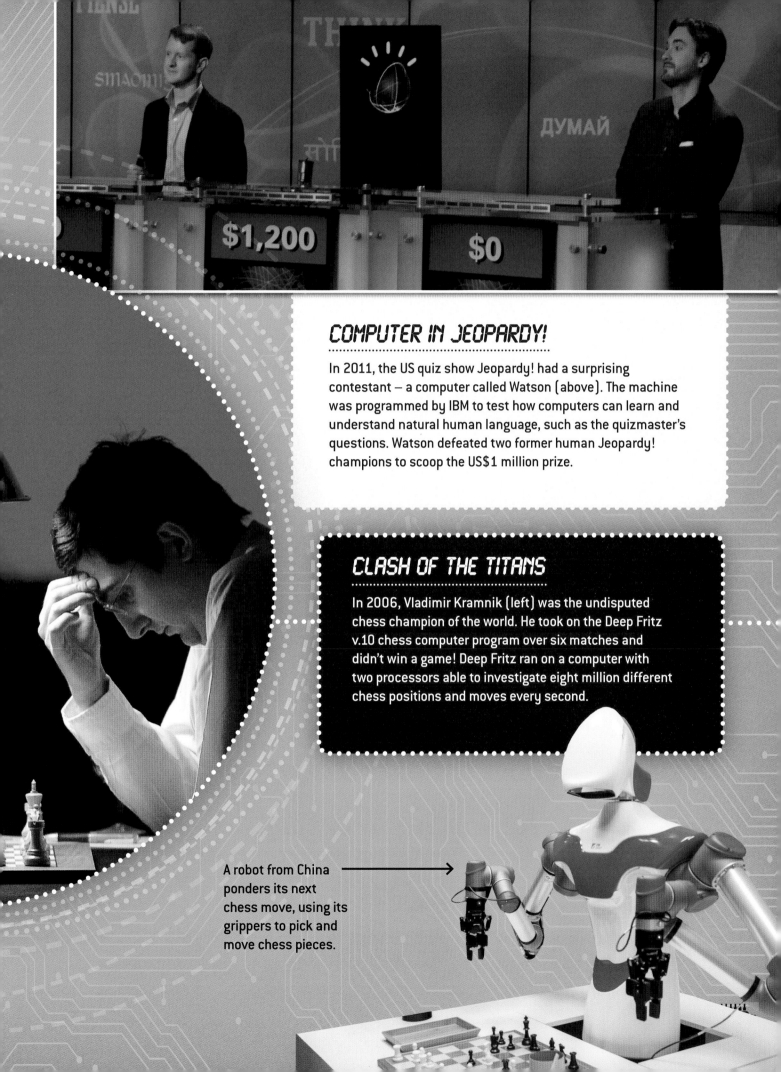

COMPUTER IN JEOPARDY!

In 2011, the US quiz show Jeopardy! had a surprising contestant – a computer called Watson (above). The machine was programmed by IBM to test how computers can learn and understand natural human language, such as the quizmaster's questions. Watson defeated two former human Jeopardy! champions to scoop the US$1 million prize.

CLASH OF THE TITANS

In 2006, Vladimir Kramnik (left) was the undisputed chess champion of the world. He took on the Deep Fritz v.10 chess computer program over six matches and didn't win a game! Deep Fritz ran on a computer with two processors able to investigate eight million different chess positions and moves every second.

A robot from China ponders its next chess move, using its grippers to pick and move chess pieces.

SMART HOMES, SMART CARS

The Internet is made up of interconnected computer networks, spanning the globe. It can be used not only by people, but also by a wide range of machines.

IN CONTROL

In a smart home, the lights, heating, cooling, televisions and other connected devices can all be controlled by a single program running on a tablet or smartphone. Users can program their lights and heating to switch on and off, record TV programmes and control many other tasks.

SMART APPLIANCES

Some Internet-connected cookers, heaters and dishwashers can communicate with each other (smart fridges can even instruct a smart cooker to switch on and heat up) and send reminders to the owner's smartphone. Some smart fridges can connect to grocery ordering services on the Internet.

HOME HELP

Personal assistants such as Amazon Echo or Google Home respond to the owner's voice instructions. Permanently connected to the Internet, the device can give news and weather forecasts, answer spoken questions via an Internet search, read audiobooks and switch other connected items on or off.

The Audi RS7 has sped round racetracks without a human driver. It uses computers and advanced navigation sensors which are accurate to within 1 cm.

DRIVERLESS CARS

The central computer in a driverless car has to take in vast amounts of inputs from sensors that detect road lanes, traffic signals and the exact positions and speeds of other vehicles. This must all be processed by the computer so that it controls the vehicle's speed and steering accurately and safely.

SMARTER CARS

Cars have long been packed with computers that control engine performance and help plot journeys. Newer cars feature computers that can alert a driver if they wander out of their lane, guide them precisely when parking safely or keep connected with smart highways for constant traffic updates.

A driverless bus in Leon, Spain

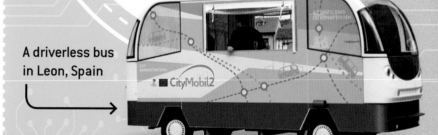

COMPUTERS IN SPACE

Space exploration uses vast amounts of computing power, but most of this remains on Earth. Space missions are run at ground control. The computing technology that controls the blast-off into space has to be stable and reliable, because the mission and sometimes astronauts' lives depend on it.

APOLLO GUIDANCE COMPUTER

Only 12 astronauts have ever set foot on the Moon. The Apollo spacecraft they travelled in was guided to its target by a computer on-board (right) that weighed over 30 kg, but had less than 64 KB of memory – less than a millionth of the memory of an Apple iPhone X!

SPACE DATA

The Hubble Space Telescope (right) orbits Earth and takes many photographs and measurements of distant stars and other bodies in space. The Hubble sends back around 210 GB of information to Earth every week, which is analysed and shared by computers on the ground.

SPACE STATION SOFTWARE

The International Space Station (ISS) is packed with computer programs that are made up of over 5.1 million lines of code. The programs run on more than 40 computers on the station and back on Earth to ensure that every part of the space station operates smoothly.

JUNO

After a five-year journey from Earth to Jupiter, the Juno space probe spent over two years orbiting the giant planet. Its RAD750 flight computer is protected inside a vault made of 1-cm-thick titanium, weighing 180 kg. The vault can withstand one million times the radiation that would kill a human being.

Italian astronaut Samantha Cristoforetti uses a tablet to help control a science experiment on board the ISS.

SPACE SIMULATORS

Before going into space, astronauts use space simulations, powered by computers, to rehearse many of the tasks their mission will require. The computers help imitate the situations they may face in space.

AUGMENTED REALITY

To augment means to add something. Augmented reality (AR) uses computer technology and coding to add elements and information to a view of the real world. Many AR applications run on people's smartphones and tablets.

MULTIMEDIA

Clicking on one of the icons or links displayed by the AR app on-screen may call up a short video about the place, or an audio soundtrack for you to listen to.

Tourist attraction

Shopping

Restaurant

Coffee Shop

KNOWING LOCATION

Many AR apps use a smartphone's global positioning system (GPS) to work out the user's precise location. They may also use the smartphone's camera to work out in which direction the user is facing. They then connect to the Internet to gather and display useful information.

ADDING LAYERS

Many AR applications add a layer of information on to a real-world scene, viewed through a smartphone or tablet's digital camera. In a tourism and travel AR app, the information may include translations of foreign language signs, or opening times of visitor attractions.

EXPERT SYSTEMS

AR apps can assist engineers and mechanics. As they view a machine to be fixed through a tablet or smartphone's camera, the app identifies parts of the machine and displays information on their fitting and repair.

TRYING THINGS OUT

AR is used in some decorating apps to see what a paint colour or piece of furniture would look like in a room, as viewed through a smartphone screen.

POKÉMON GO

A gaming sensation when it was released in 2016, Pokémon Go is an augmented reality game where players roam their neighbourhood, seeking out Pokémon characters. The aim is to catch, train and battle the characters with others at places known as 'gyms'.

VIRTUAL REALITY

Virtual reality (VR) places a person inside an environment generated by computers that appears realistic. The person can move around in this virtual world and interact with the objects it contains.

ENTERING A NEW WORLD

Some virtual reality systems surround a user with large screens, but many applications run on headsets like this PlayStation VR (below). Virtual reality games and experiences thrust the user right into the centre of the action.

3D WORLD

Hypersuit VR platforms (above) can be paired with a VR headset to create an exciting free-flying virtual reality experience. A complete environment is projected on to the inside of the headset the user wears. As they turn their head, the computer-generated scene changes just as it would if they were looking around in their actual environment.

HMD

The head mounted display (HMD) projects two slightly different views of the same scene in front of the user's eyes. Just like when viewing a regular scene, the brain merges these two views to gain a three dimensional (3D) image.

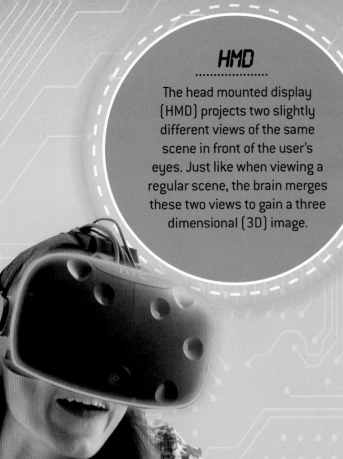

VR USES

Virtual Reality is great for 3D gaming and fun experiences, but it also has a serious side. Engineers, architects, military personnel, doctors, dentists and astronauts all use VR systems to train and rehearse difficult tasks.

CONTROLS

The platform tilts and moves with the user who controls their flying direction by moving their arms. Other VR systems use gloves containing sensors which detect hand movement and pressure.

TRANSPORT SIMULATORS

Flight simulators for pilot training are entire flight decks with all the controls found in a real aircraft. Many are placed on top of a platform which can be tilted and moved to simulate the physical feeling of the plane climbing, banking and diving.

FUTURE COMPUTING

Computing has changed fast – 30 years ago, for example, there were no smartphones or streaming videos, and the World Wide Web didn't exist. So what will the next 30 or more years bring?

COMPUTERS IN CONTROL

More and more computing will find its way into other machines, making them smarter and able to work by themselves. Expect to see more intelligent robots in everyday life, as well as driverless vehicles and smart cities where buildings, signs and street lighting can recognise, track and assist you.

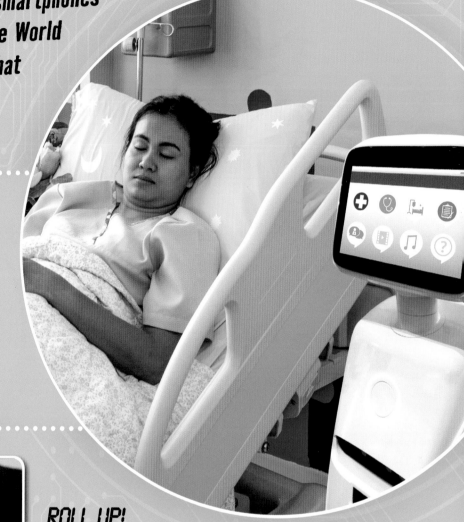

ROLL UP!

Nanotechnology (see below) and other advances may lead to large, flexible electronic displays that you can roll or fold up and place in your pocket. Augmented reality may do away with a physical display altogether, projecting everything on to a virtual screen in front of you.

NANOCOMPUTING

Nanotechnology is the science and engineering of really small things, measured in nanometres – a billionth of a metre. Nanocomputing could shrink computing technology down to handfuls of atoms in size. In future, computers the size of your finger might have as much power as today's biggest supercomputers!

Supermodel Karolina Kurkova wears a smart dress which features 150 LED lights. These change colour according to real-time likes and other reactions from social media users.

ALWAYS ON
....

Advances in battery technology and energy efficiency could lead to more portable computing. This technology will be part of what you wear every day, and will always be with you. It might be powered by your body movements, with sensors and processors monitoring your health, location and any tasks you need to carry out.

SMART CLOTHING
....

Pioneering smart clothes created by AiQ contain sensors to monitor your body's health. Other smart clothes will provide touchscreens on sleeves that can be swiped and pressed to control a smartphone.

MIND OVER MATTER
....

All input and commands to future computers may be by thoughts alone. In 2017, MIT CSAIL demonstrated a robot that could be controlled by a person's brain signals, picked up by an Electroencephalogram (EEG) cap worn on the head. It might even lead to neurogaming, where players control their in-game characters

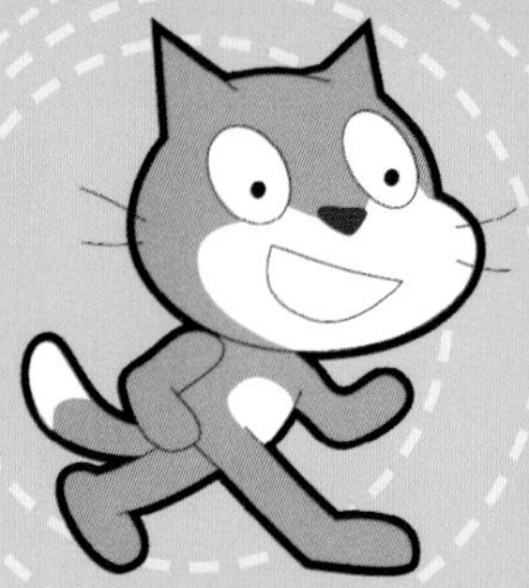

MAKE YOUR OWN SCRATCH GAME

Scratch is a fun yet powerful computer programming language. It uses colour-coded blocks that you drag and drop into part of the screen, called the 'scripting area', to form a program.

LET'S GET STARTED

Start out by visiting https://scratch.mit.edu . Find the 'Getting Started with Scratch' tutorial by clicking on 'Create' and then looking in the 'Tips' menu. This will teach you how to save and run a Scratch program, as well as basics about how to use the coding blocks.

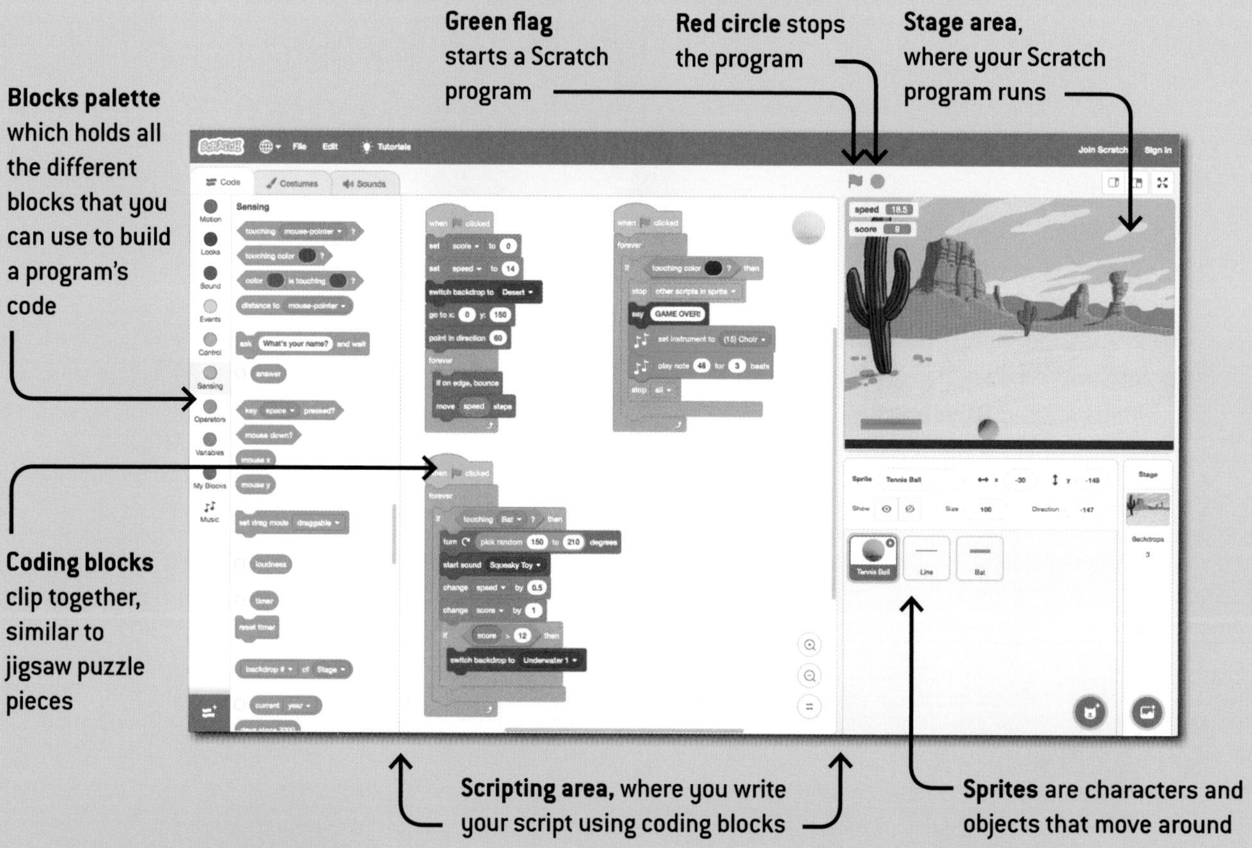
Green flag starts a Scratch program
Red circle stops the program
Stage area, where your Scratch program runs
Blocks palette which holds all the different blocks that you can use to build a program's code
Coding blocks clip together, similar to jigsaw puzzle pieces
Scripting area, where you write your script using coding blocks
Sprites are characters and objects that move around

DESERT PONG

You're going to code a simple Pong game that can be played using a mouse to move the bat left and right. The aim will be to use the bat to avoid the ball crossing the red line. This is similar to the early computer games that were played in the 1970s (see page 28).

1. MAKE YOUR SPRITES

You need three sprites that will interact in the game.

Delete the cat sprite and click on the 'Choose a Sprite' icon (the blue circle).

Scroll through the different sprites available and select the tennis ball. It should pop up in your sprites panel. Go back and repeat. This time, select the red line sprite.

Head back to 'Choose new Sprite' a third time and select the green paddle sprite. Once it is in your sprites panel, click on it and rename the paddle, 'bat'.

2. BACKGROUND SETTING

You can pick a background for your game. Head to the Stage area and click on the blue circle which is the 'Choose a Backdrop' icon. A series of different backgrounds will be displayed. Select the desert scene. Repeat and, this time, pick the Underwater 1 scene.

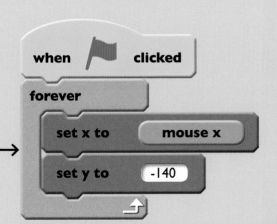

3. IN POSITION

The start of your Scratch program needs to set the positions of the bat and the red line. Click on your bat sprite and start dragging blocks over to the script panel. These are all colour-coded. Look for the yellow commands of the 'events' section, and drag your first block over.

Go to 'control' to select a 'forever' block. This creates a program loop, so that any command inside its jaws is repeated until the game ends. This block can snap on to the bottom of your first one. Now, head to the 'motion' section (dark blue) and drag over a 'set x' and a 'set y' block. You will use these to set the coordinates where the bat will be at the start of the game.

For 'set y', click on the small window and type '-140'. This command now places the bat at the bottom of the screen.

Go to the 'sensing' (light blue) section and drag the 'mouse x' block over to your scripts panel. Place it over the '0' in the 'set x' block to lock it in. Make sure the box starts glowing before you drop it in. Move the blocks into the 'forever' loop, and you should end up with the following:

4. CROSSING THE LINE

Click on your 'line' sprite and build a script that sets the red line as running along the bottom of your game screen. ————————————

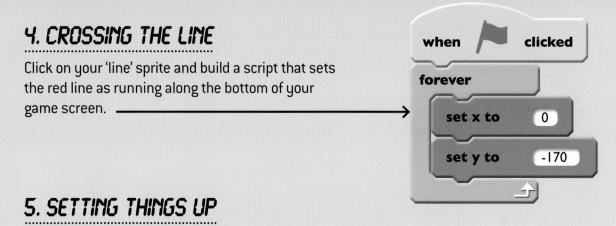

5. SETTING THINGS UP

Now, the real coding can begin! You need to click on your ball sprite and start dragging blocks over to create the script below.

First, you need to create two variables. These are counters used to keep track of important numbers in the game. Go to the orange set of block commands ('variables') and click 'make a variable'. Give it the name 'speed' and click 'ok'. Repeat, to make another variable, this time with the name 'score'.

Now, when you go to the 'variables' commands, you can drag over 'set speed' and 'set score' blocks. Select the variable you need by clicking on the down arrow and selecting from the drop-down menu.

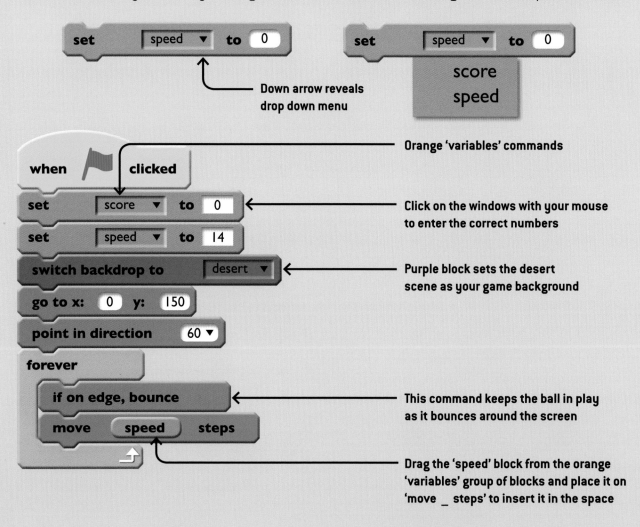

6. BATTING IT BACK

Let's take a look at how to produce the script that makes the ball bounce off the bat.
You can add a few other features to your game while coding this, too.

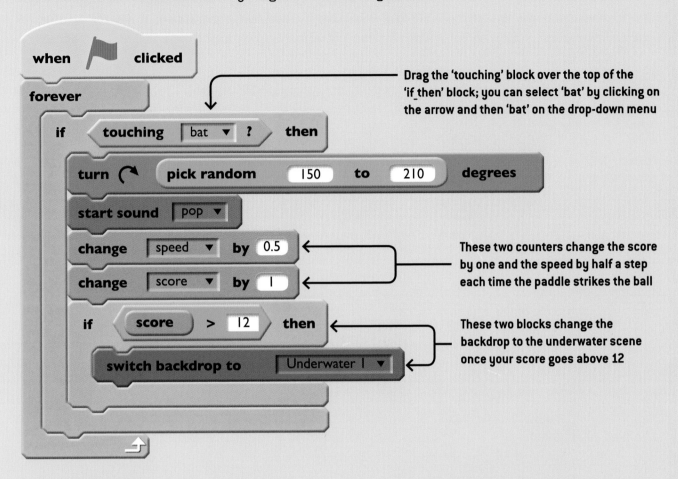

Drag the 'touching' block over the top of the 'if_then' block; you can select 'bat' by clicking on the arrow and then 'bat' on the drop-down menu

These two counters change the score by one and the speed by half a step each time the paddle strikes the ball

These two blocks change the backdrop to the underwater scene once your score goes above 12

7. GAME OVER!

You're nearly there. The final script you have to build deals with what happens if the ball touches the red line. This involves adding the music extension by clicking the 'Add Extension' icon in the bottom left corner and clicking 'Music'.

The 'touching color' block has a handy feature. You can change the colour it tries to detect, simply by clicking on its square of colour and selecting the pipette. Then, move your cursor around the screen and click on the colour you want.

Drag the 'say' block over to your scripts, delete 'Hello!' and type in 'GAME OVER!'

Pick instrument '(15) Choir' from the drop-down menu (or any instrument you prefer)

'Stop all' block ends the program

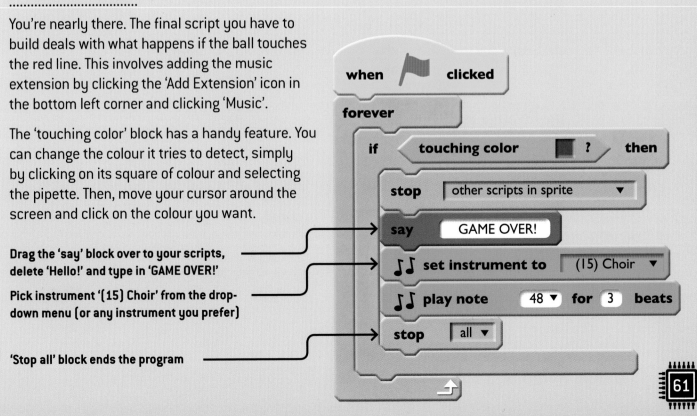

61

8. GAME ON

Save the project and run the game by pressing the green flag at the top of the screen. You can move the paddle left and right using your mouse. The ball should drop down at an angle and bounce back up at an angle when it strikes your bat. Each time you hit the ball, one point is added to your score and the ball speeds up a little. Can you keep the ball in play long enough for the desert background to turn into an underwater scene?

9. CREATIVE CODING

You can customise parts of this basic game by changing the scripts or adding new ones. How would you alter or improve the game? Here are some starting points. Remember to save your work regularly and keep a spare copy of the original game in case you want to start again.

Try out different backdrops. Make new backgrounds and, in the first ball script, alter the 'switch backdrop' block to your new background's name.

Experiment with different sounds from the Sound Library (accessible by clicking on the 'sounds' tab at the top of the screen, and then the speaker symbol). Try adding the 'cave' or the 'jungle' sound to the end of the game. You can do this by removing the two greeny-blue commands from the third script and simply adding the 'start sound' block.

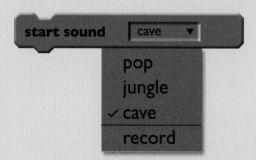

To make the game harder, you can set a faster starting speed, or increase the speed by 0.75 or 1 every time it hits the bat, rather than 0.5.

Add a bonus score of 10 points when the game switches to the underwater background by adding this block underneath 'switch backdrop' in the second script.

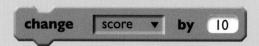

Enjoy playing and customising your very own Pong game!

GLOSSARY

binary The base-two number system made up of just ones and zeroes.

circuit A path along which an electric signal can be carried.

code The language that programmers create and use to tell a computer what to do.

compiler A program which converts instruction into code that the computer's processor understands.

gigabyte (GB) A measure of memory, with one gigabyte equalling 1,024 megabytes (MB).

HTML Short for HyperText Markup Language, this is a type of language that web pages are written in, so that they can be displayed on different devices accessing the Internet.

Internet A network of computer networks that connects millions of computers all over the world.

kilobyte (KB) A measure of memory, with one kilobyte equalling 1,024 bytes.

megabyte (MB) A measure of memory, with one megabyte equalling 1,024 kilobytes (KB).

megaflop A measure of speed of a computer. One megaflop equals one million floating point operations per second.

network Two or more computers or digital devices linked together so that they can communicate with one another.

operating system A computer program that runs a computer's basic functions and manages other programs running on the system.

processor The part of a computer, usually made up of a chip packed with electronic circuits, which performs tasks and instructs other parts of the computer.

program A series of instructions written in code which allow a computer to perform a task.

Random access memory (RAM) A type of computer memory used to store data temporarily. It can be overwritten with new data but empties when power is switched off.

resolution The number of tiny blocks of colour (called pixels) found on a display.

simulator A program or system which mimics realistically another setting such as flying a plane or performing an operation.

terabyte (TB) A measure of memory, with one terabyte equalling 1,027 gigabytes (GB).

transistor Tiny electronic components which can act as switches and amplifiers in a circuit.

web server A computer that stores and serves up (delivers) web pages to viewers when they are connected to the Internet and they make a request.

World Wide Web (WWW) A massive system of information available on the Internet, made up of millions of documents and images all linked together.

FURTHER INFORMATION

Books

Adventures in STEAM: Computers by Claudia Martin (Wayland, 2017)

Get Ahead in Computing: The Science of Computers by Clive Gifford (Wayland, 2015)

Project Code: Create Computer Games with Scratch by Kevin Wood (Franklin Watts, 2017)

Computing and Programming by Shahneila Saeed (Wayland, 2015)

The Quick Expert's Guide to Computing and Programming by Shahneila Saeed (Wayland, 2016)

Websites

www.computerhistory.org/timeline/computers/
A large and detailed illustrated timeline of computers.

www.bbc.co.uk/guides/z2tgr82
Learn lots about digital images and graphics at this BBC Bitesize site.

www.onsite-computers.co.uk/play-zx-spectrum-games-online.html
Have fun playing realistic 1980s ZX Spectrum games on this website.

INDEX

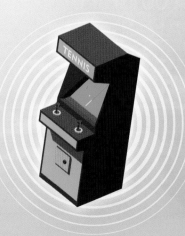